YOU ARE AWESOME

21 CRAFTS
TO MAKE YOU HAPPY

ABBEY HENDRICKSON

Contents

Introduction

You are awesome! Don't you wish people told you that more often?
I certainly do. These 21 craft projects were originally made for my
favorite people – the ones who make me laugh; the ones who
are interesting, clever, and smart; the ones who raise a glass with
me to celebrate a good day; the ones I turn to when I'm sad; the
ones who make my life that little bit more awesome.

Five years ago, with encouragement from a co-worker and while
expecting my first baby, I started writing a blog called Aesthetic
Outburst. It started out being, as some blogs do, the complete opposite of
awesome. It was dull and uninspired. Baby this, job that... I'd throw in
an occasional craft project, but for the most part... ugh, yawn! Things
started to shift once I decided to take a risk and leave my job at an art
museum to head to graduate school for Visual Studies. With my husband
and our three-week-old baby in tow, we picked up and moved to Buffalo,
New York. I quickly fell head over heels in love with Buffalo. Something
about that raw, once-industrial city made my heart beat faster, motivated
me. Enthusiasm is contagious and I'm convinced that my mint condition
eagerness resulted in an intuitive, but critical shift, both in life and on
my blog. Living in a new city with my little family, making craft projects,
documenting long, rambling walks, baking cookies for our 90-year-old
landlord, decorating our fabulous old apartment, eating good food and
drinking good wine with incredible friends... it all seeped onto Aesthetic
Outburst and people started to take notice. As I started to connect with
a supportive community of fellow bloggers and blog readers, I found
myself feeling energized and lucky.

Right after finishing graduate school, and hugely pregnant with our
second baby, the college where my husband taught laid off their non-
tenured faculty. To our dismay, the lay-off included my husband. Over the
years, we had waveringly spoken about moving back to the rural town
where I grew up to be closer to our families, but until that moment, it had
never been in earnest. We were shocked when a "someday" idea became a
forced reality. We moved to Owego, New York, four hours south of Buffalo.

You know that saying, 'go big or go home'? I'm living proof that,
sometimes, it's best to go home. Because when you do, sometimes that
something big just may happen. Admittedly, moving back to my rural

hometown was not an easy transition. I kept blogging, but found myself at home with two babies, struggling to keep us occupied on a daily basis. Elaborate forts, cardboard spaceships, and woodland animal costumes seemed like the best answer.

On a whim, I called one of my closest friends and pitched the idea of me making one craft project each weekday and giving all of the work away to blog readers. She laughed and told me I was crazy, but encouraged me to go ahead. So, I did. I started out re-creating projects I'd already made and given to my favorite people. The biggest surprise was that the ideas kept flowing, one generating the next, striking in the oddest of places. Wandering the aisles of our local hardware store... IDEA! Watching fireworks... IDEA! Mowing the lawn... IDEA! I made tons of craft projects – costumes, ornaments, and valentines. Some turned out great and others were absolute disasters. The successful projects got sent out into the world, but oddly enough, it was the disasters that I found myself living for. I never knew when a bad craft project would set me on a path to something really good; something I couldn't have imagined without a near catastrophe. Every inch of our house was covered in craft materials. Within five months, I had given away 80 handmade projects to strangers and my once-dull little blog started moving more towards awesome, more towards what I hoped it could be.

From a very young age, I've wanted to be an artist and write a book. Did I ever think it would happen? No, not really. It was with the help of remarkably supportive readers, a wonderful blogging community, and my long-suffering family, that a creative risk turned into an actual opportunity. I've always said that what I love most about making art is getting lost in it, those moments when you don't realize how much time has passed. It feels like going to a movie theater during the day; you know, when you emerge from the dark theater and the sun's still bright and shining... it's fabulous. That's my hope for you – that you take risks, that you be authentic and put yourself out there, that you get lost in making something for someone, that you get in trouble and make some disasters, that you meet friends who make you incandescently happy, and that you enjoy it all because you are awesome!

ABBEY HENDRICKSON

Projects

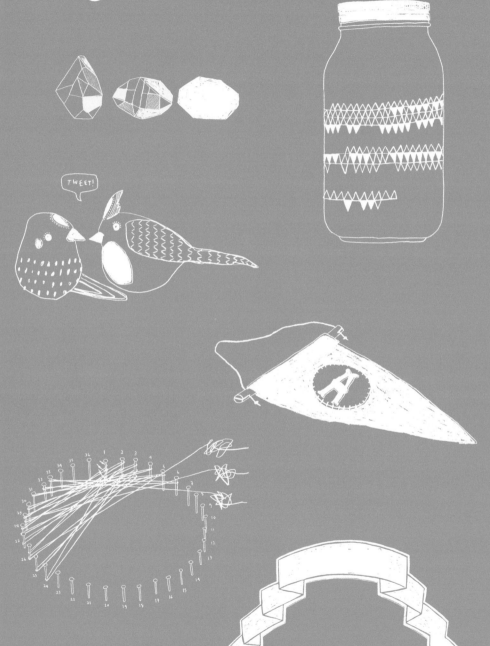

Ribbon Chalkboard

A banner to hang above a favorite photo or print? A welcome sign for your door? Your choice.

Materials

» **wood**
» **extra-fine opaque white paint pen**
» **chalkboard paint**
» **sawtooth picture hanging hardware**

Tools

» **tacky glue**
» **pencil**
» **jigsaw**
» **safety glasses**
» **sandpaper**
» **paintbrush**
» **ribbon template (see p. 73)**

What to do

1. Photocopy the template and enlarge it so that it measures roughly 12" x 7" (or make it larger if you so wish).
2. Trace the template onto your piece of wood with a pencil.
3. Wearing safety glasses, carefully cut the shape from the wood using a jigsaw.
4. Sand down the rough edges and use a damp cloth to remove any sawdust.
5. Paint the top of the wood with chalkboard paint and allow to dry.
6. Use sandpaper to remove any stray paint.
7. Draw lines along the edge using a paint pen and allow to dry.
8. Center the picture hanging hardware on the back of the chalkboard and secure with tacky glue.
9. Allow to dry and write your mesaage!

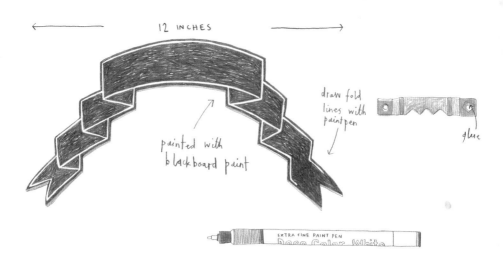

12 INCHES

painted with blackboard paint

draw fold lines with paint pen

glue

EXTRA FINE PAINT PEN
Deco Color White

Spirograph Decoration

Banish the black velvet and replace it with unfinished wood and copper nails. Not quite as 70's, but still cool.

Materials

» **wood**
» **small copper nails**
» **3 skeins of embroidery thread in different colors**

Tools

» **pencil**
» **ruler**
» **hammer**
» **scissors**
» **saw**
» **sandpaper**
» **safety glasses**
» **drill with small bit**
» **clear nail polish**
» **circle template (see p. 74)**

What to do

1. Wearing safety glasses, saw the wood into a 5" x 5" square and sand down the rough edges.
2. On the back of the wood, mark a point at the center, 1" from the top, and drill a hole at the mark, being careful not to drill through the wood. Sand down any rough edges.
3. Photocopy the template and enlarge it so that it measures 4½" in diameter.
4. Flip the wood over, place the template in the center of the square, and lightly trace around it, marking the 36 dots along its edge.
5. Hammer a nail at each mark, being careful not to drive any nails through the wood.
6. Select the first thread color and tie a knot around the top nail (nail #1).
7. From nail #1, bring the thread to nail #24, wrap it around that nail and bring it to nail #2. Go from there to #25, then to #3, then to #26, etc. in a clockwise direction. Knot at #1 when you've completed the first thread color.
8. Select the next thread color and tie it to nail #1. Bring to nail #26, then to nail #2, then nail #27, etc. knotting when finished.
9. Select the final thread color and tie it to nail #1. Bring to nail #28, etc. knotting at the end.
10. Secure each knot with a drop of nail polish and allow to dry.
11. Carefully trim any long threads as close to the knots as possible.

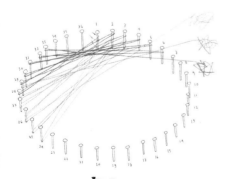

move in a clockwise direction

WHOSE HAIR?

CHRISTINA CHRISTOFOROU

WOCHENENDE
spefekte falsfekte sep

JUST KIDS | PATTI SMITH

A5/04 KELLER WOCHE

MÜLLER 'ELAND 1967 - 03 '

Kelse
Woch

LARS MÜLLER PUBLISHERS

THE ART BOOK

Φ

OWNING ART
THE CONTEMPORARY ART COLLECTOR'S HANDBOOK

OWNING ART

Frost*

WHY BLACK?

GI

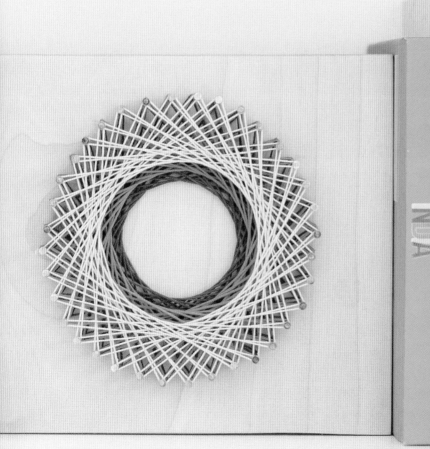

Awesome Pegs

Tell someone special how awesome they are! These would be a fun surprise on a door or cubicle – just print out some favorite photos and use these clips to hang them on a string.

Materials
- » **17 wood spring clothespins**
- » **17 dimensional letters (available at craft stores)**
- » **acrylic paint**

Tools
- » **paintbrush**
- » **sandpaper**
- » **tacky glue**

What to do
1. Paint the top of each clothespin and allow the paint to dry.
2. Sand the clothespin edges to remove any stray paint.
3. Apply tacky glue to the back of each letter and position the letter at the top, painted side of each clothespin. Allow to dry before using.

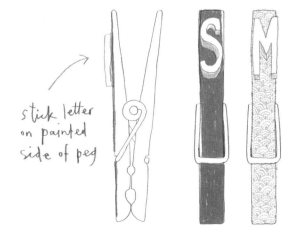

stick letter on painted side of peg

cover the back of the letter with glue

Rainbow Necklace

Who wouldn't be happy wearing a rainbow around their neck all day?

Materials

- » **20" length of necklace wire, 24 gauge**
- » **acrylic paint in the following colors: dark blue, turquoise, light blue, green, yellow, light orange, orange, pink, red**
- » **18 unfinished wooden beads 1" diameter (available at most craft stores)**
- » **matt acrylic sealer spray**
- » **jump-ring jewelry component**
- » **spring-ring jewelry component**
- » **2 small beads**
- » **2mm crimp tube beads**

Tools

- » **pliers**
- » **skewers**
- » **paintbrush**

What to do

1. Thread the wooden beads onto skewers, leaving a bit of space between each.
2. Rest the skewers on boxes of some sort, making sure the beads do not touch any surface.
3. Cover each bead in two coats of acrylic paint, allowing the paint to dry in between coats.
4. Once dry, leave the beads on the skewers and coat them with acrylic sealer spray. Allow to dry completely.
5. Attach the jump-ring to the necklace wire. Thread the crimp tube bead and use pliers to crimp.
6. Thread everything on in the following order: smallest bead, big wooden beads, the other small bead, another crimp tube bead, and the spring-ring.
7. Wrap the necklace wire back through the crimp tube bead, the small bead and one big bead. Crimp the crimp tube bead and trim the necklace wire.

18 large beads   small bead   crimp   spring ring

small bead   jump ring
crimp
crimp   spring ring   small bead

Geometric Ornament

Quite possibly the easiest handmade ornament you'll ever make. Ever.

What to do

1. Take a block and lay your ruler from corner to corner on one of its sides. Lightly draw a line with a pencil.
2. Repeat for all sides.
3. Carefully paint each triangle, allowing each side to dry in between painting.
4. Lightly sand the edges of the block.
5. Once the block is dry, pre-drill a small hole in one corner.
6. Apply a dab of tacky glue on the end of the screw eye and screw it into the corner, wiping away any excess glue.
7. Once the glue has dried, thread a string or ribbon through the screw eye to hang the ornament.

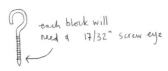

each block will need a 17/32" screw eye

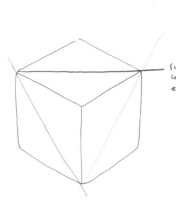

rule lines from corner to corner on each side of the cube

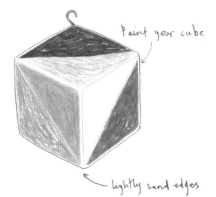

Paint your cube

lightly sand edges

Embroidery Names

This was a wedding gift for our friends, but you could embroider your name with your sweetheart's, your kids' names, your two goldfish, anything – two lines, one heart.

Materials
» **needlework fabric**
» **3 skeins of embroidery thread in different colors**
» **embroidery hoop**

Tools
» **needle**
» **scissors**
» **masking tape**
» **font pattern (see p. 75)**

What to do

1. Secure the needlework fabric in the embroidery hoop.
2. To prevent fraying, apply masking tape along the edges of the needlework fabric.
3. Choose your text and use the font pattern as reference.
4. Starting from the back, use a half cross-stitch to stitch your message on the needlework fabric, making sure that all of the stitches are going in the same direction.
5. Rather than making knots, secure the thread by tucking it in on itself. Use this method to add new thread.
6. Once your design is complete, carefully trim and discard any excess needlework fabric.
7. Leave it in the embroidery hoop for display.

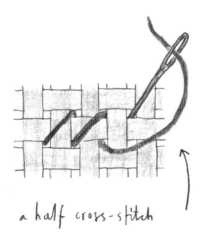

a half cross-stitch

Lo-Fi Laptop

Add some alphabet and number stickers to the keys to help your little one learn her letters and numbers while they're clacking away on their laptop.

- » 1 slim cardboard box with a lid (I used an empty 100-sheet resumé paper box)
- » 1 roll silver duct tape
- » masking or washi tape in a variety of colors
- » fun stickers
- » small alphabet and numeral stickers
- » black acrylic paint

- » scissors
- » paintbrush

What to do

1. To make the screen, paint the inside of the cardboard box and allow to dry.
2. Cover the outside of both parts of the box with strips of duct tape, being sure to fold the tape so that it covers the edges, but not the inside.
3. Trim the tape at the corners to reduce bulkiness.
4. Cut 51 strips of masking tape in a variety of sizes for the keyboard.
5. Cut a 3" x 2" piece of masking tape and two small strips of a different tape for the mouse pad.
6. Apply alphabet and numeral stickers to the keyboard.
7. Apply stickers and masking tape on the right and left sides of the screen in the pattern of your computer icons.
8. Tuck the keyboard into the screen. Leave it unglued so the little one can open and close the cardboard laptop freely.

51 different size strips of tape for the keyboard

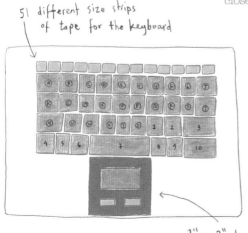

masking tapes

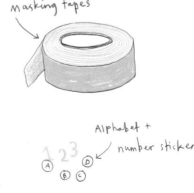

3" x 2" tape for mouse pad

Alphabet + number stickers

Natural Magnets

Finally, a set of alphabet magnets that you won't mind picking up off the kitchen floor 100 times a day.

What to do

1. Cut your stick into 26 pieces, each approximately 1" thick.
2. After cutting, allow the twig pieces to dry completely.
3. Center one alphabet sticker on each twig piece.
4. Paint directly over the stickers (the stickers will act as a resist).
5. Remove the stickers and discard.
6. Wait for the paint to dry and then glue a magnet to the back of each twig.

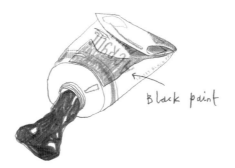

Black paint

Slices of wood ↑

magnet

Alphabet stickers

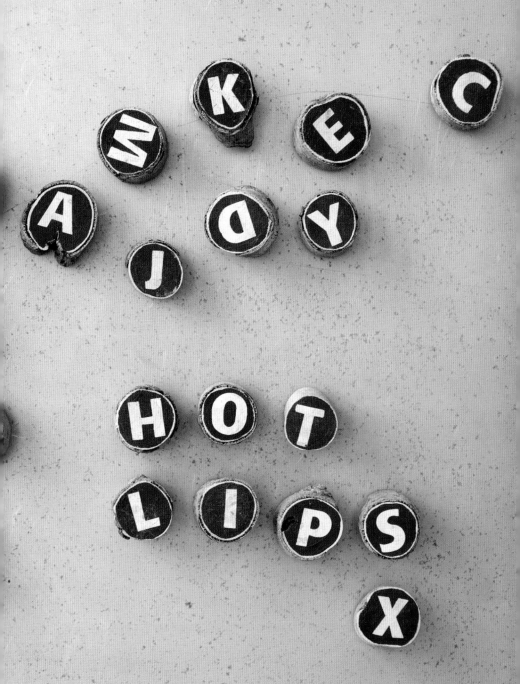

Faceted Necklace

Go ahead and make it for yourself. We both know you'll rock it.

Materials

» **1 small package of black Fimo clay (to make 8 medium-sized beads)**
» **parchment paper**
» **silver ball chain necklace**

Tools

» **exacto knife with a sharp blade**
» **wooden skewer**
» **oven**
» **baking sheet**

CUT
CARVE
SHAVE
CHIP

your beads will catch the light

What to do

1. Break off a small piece of the clay and knead until it's pliable. The size depends on the bead size you're aiming for, but make it a bit bigger than the final bead you'd like, as you'll be shaving off some of the clay.
2. Roll the clay into a ball and flatten it slightly.
3. Carefully twist the wooden skewer into the clay from one side until you can see it poking through. Remove the skewer and poke it into the hole from the opposite side. This will make your holes cleaner. If the holes do have rough edges, just use your finger to smooth them out.
4. Repeat this for as many beads as you'd like to make.
5. Place a sheet of parchment on a cookie sheet and carefully set your beads on it.
6. Following the directions on the package, bake your beads.
7. Once your beads have cooled completely, use your exacto knife to carve into the clay, shaving away small sections at a time. You may want to use a self-healing mat underneath your work area.
8. The knife will create striations in the clay going in the same direction as your cuts. Change the direction of your cuts in order to change the striations.
9. Thread your beads onto the ball chain necklace.

shiny looking gem stones

Envelope Notebooks

Packaged with some stamps and a few fun pencils, these books make a great gift for a little friend about to travel.

Materials

- » **1 security envelope**
- » **string**
- » **10 sheets of blank paper**
- » **masking or washi tape**

Tools

- » **scissors**
- » **needle**
- » **bone folder or folding tool**
- » **ruler**
- » **exacto knife with a sharp blade**
- » **pencil**

What to do

1. Seal the envelope closed.
2. Once dry, trim the envelope along three edges and reverse the fold so that the inside pattern is facing outwards.
3. Trim the envelope so it measures 5¾" x 3½", making sure not to cut the folded edge.
4. Use a bone folder or an alternative folding tool to fold the blank pages crisply in half.
5. Cut the pages down to 5¾" x 3½" (you may have to trim them slightly smaller to fit).
6. Stack the folded pages inside one another and tuck them into the envelope so that they form a book.
7. Open to the center spread in the book and mark three holes at the crease, one ½" from the top, one in the center, and one ½" from the bottom.
8. Use a needle to poke a hole at each mark.
9. Thread the needle and, from the inside, push through the center hole, leaving a 3" thread tail inside. Be sure to hold the book together firmly while you do this.
10. Holding the thread tail in place with one finger, push the needle through the top hole of the spine and sew back inside the book.
11. Push out the bottom hole and thread back in the center hole, making sure that there is a tail on either side of the thread.
12. Pull tight, make a knot with the tails, and cut the excess thread (not too close to the knot).
13. If any folded paper is sticking out, carefully trim it back.
14. Cover the spine with a 5¾" strip of colored tape.

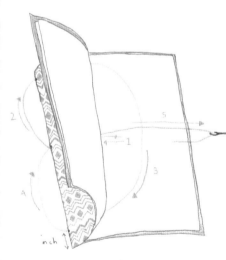

Ring Toss

Hang your ring toss game and have fun making up crazy rules!

Materials

» **¾" thick wood**
» **acrylic paint**
» **13 cup hooks**
» **sawtooth picture hanging hardware**
» **extra-fine paint pen (optional)**
» **several 3" rubber rings (look in the plumbing aisle)**

Tools

» **jigsaw**
» **safety glasses**
» **pencil**
» **sandpaper**
» **paintbrush**
» **graphite transfer paper**
» **ring toss template (see p. 76)**

What to do

1. Photocopy the template so that it measures 17" x 14", and trace it onto the wood with a pencil.
2. Wearing safety glasses, use a jigsaw to cut out the shield shape and sand down any rough edges.
3. Lay a sheet of graphite transfer paper directly onto the wood (graphite side down) and the ring toss template (facing up) on top of the graphite paper. Trace over the numbers with a pencil, transferring them onto the surface of the wood.
4. Use a small paintbrush to paint each number. Allow to dry.
5. For further definition, you can use the paint pen to carefully trace along the edge of each number. Allow to dry.
6. Screw one cup hook above each numeral (you may want to pre-drill holes. If so, be careful not to drill through the wood).
7. On the back of the game, secure the sawtooth picture hanging hardware at the top center.

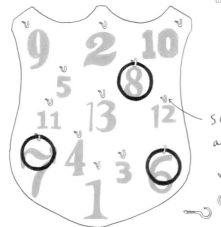

screw a cup-hook above each numeral

41

Pennant

Kick it old school with this vintage-inspired felt pennant.

Materials

» **3 pieces of felt in different colors**
» **thread**
» **wooden dowel**

Tools

» **scissors**
» **pencil**
» **ruler**
» **needle**
» **exacto knife and blade**
» **straight pins**

What to do

1. Measure and cut out a 12" x 30" x 30" triangle from felt.
2. Using a mug or a small plate as a template, cut out a felt circle measuring 5" diameter.
3. Find a font you like and print out a letter on cardstock. Trace the letter onto the felt and cut it out.
4. Center the felt letter on the 5" felt circle and attach with a straight stitch.
5. Place the circle on the felt triangle and use a blanket stitch to attach it.
6. Fold down the top 2" of the triangle and tack with straight pins to make a pocket.
7. Sew along the raw edge of the pocket and trim off the small triangles at either end.
8. Using a sharp exacto knife, very carefully make notches in each end of the dowel rod and slide it into the pocket.
9. To hang, knot the thread on each end and slide it into the dowel rod notches.

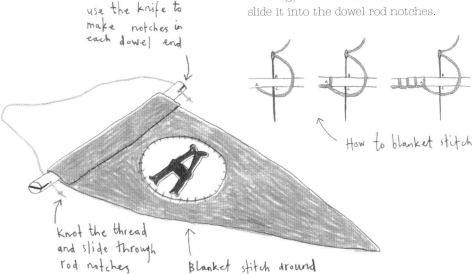

use the knife to make notches in each dowel end

How to blanket stitch

Knot the thread and slide through rod notches

Blanket stitch around the circle

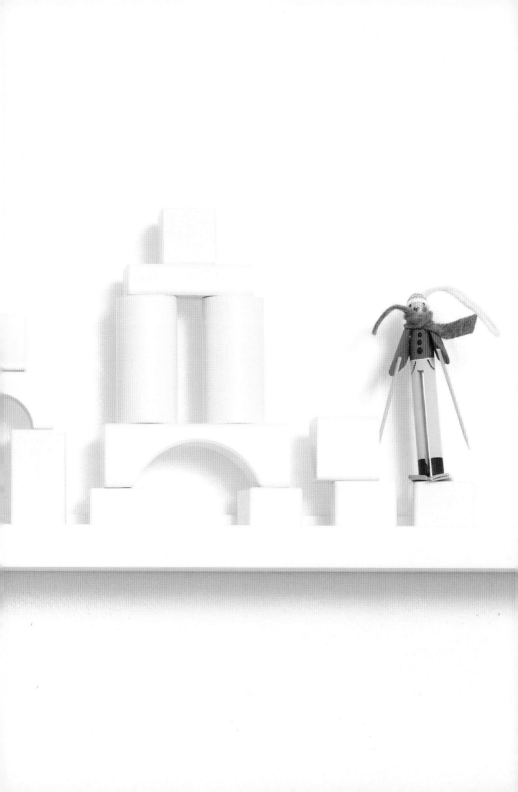

Clothespin Skier

Everyone deserves a holiday now and then, right? Make this ski bunny as a reminder.

Materials

» **2 traditional wooden clothespins**
» **acrylic paint in yellow, orange, pink, light blue, and black**
» **puff paint in pink, white, and black**
» **miniature pompom**
» **2 wooden toothpicks**
» **1 popsicle stick**
» **string**
» **small piece of felt**
» **fine-tipped permanent black marker**

Tools

» **sandpaper**
» **exacto knife and blade or small saw**
» **small paintbrush**
» **tacky glue**

What to do

1. Using a small saw or sharp exacto knife, cut the two bottom, slanted pieces off of the first clothespin. Each piece should measure approximately 1½". Lightly sand any rough edges and set aside.

2. Now for the arms: On the second clothespin, trim off the two pieces just where the edges start to slant. Lightly sand any rough edges.

3. For the poles, clip off one end of each of the two toothpicks, leaving one pointed side. Lightly sand any rough edges.

4. Paint the ski pants, coat, boots, and hat on the longer clothespin. Allow paint to dry.

5. Paint the coat arms and mittens on the two small clothespin pieces (with slanted edges). Allow paint to dry.

6. Use a fine black pen to draw details on the hat, pants, and mittens.

7. Apply buttons, facial features, and the hat rim with the puff paint and allow the paint to dry.

8. Glue the arm pieces onto the body with tacky glue and allow to dry.

9. For the skis, cut the popsicle stick in half and sand any rough edges.

10. Glue one popsicle stick half to each foot and glue one toothpick to each hand.

11. Cut a little piece of felt so it measures ¼" x 4" and knot it around your skier's neck.

12. Cut a 4" length of string and glue it on the back to hang.

SKIER

Wooden clothespins

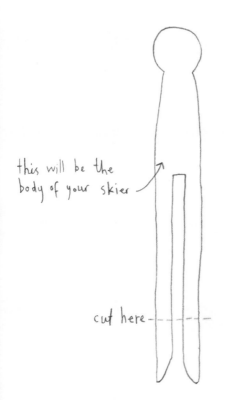

this will be the
body of your skier

cut here - - - - - - -

minature
pompom

paint the body
and arms

Your skier's now
ready for the
mountain slopes

ROCKY
MOUNTAINS

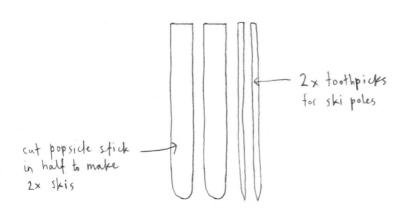

2x toothpicks
for ski poles

cut popsicle stick
in half to make
2x skis

Drink Markers

Start planning your next party! Need to remember which drink is yours or do you just need to remember how many drinks you've had? If cocktails aren't your thing, these could also be used to hold notes or photos on a string.

Materials

» **(10) 1" wood circles (available from most DIY stores)**
» **10 miniature spring clothespins**
» **black acrylic paint**
» **extra-fine opaque white paint pen**

Tools

» **paintbrush**
» **sandpaper**
» **tacky glue**

What to do

1. Paint the top of each wooden circle and allow to dry.
2. Sand the edges to remove any stray paint.
3. Use the paint pen to draw small dots along the edge and a number in the center of each. Allow the paint to dry.
4. Glue one wooden circle to the top of each clothespin, making sure the numbers are visible.

10 x 1" wood circles
10 x miniature pegs

use paint pen to decorate and add numbers

ACRYLIC Paint

Paint the top of each circle

stick miniature pegs to the back

EXTRA FINE PAINT PEN
Deco Color White

Stitched Screen Door

The front door of our old farmhouse went from sad to happy once I sewed a big, welcoming hello on it.

Materials

» **pet-proof screen kit (or existing screen)**
» **3 skeins of embroidery thread**

Tools

» **needle**
» **scissors**
» **tape measure**
» **masking tape**
» **hello template (see p. 77)**

What to do

1. Assemble the screen according to the package instructions or use a cleaned, pre-existing screen.
2. Photocopy the template and enlarge it. I used it so that it measured 19" across, 12" high, and had a ¾" space between each letter. However, the size and grid of your screen will dictate your stitch count, so adapt it accordingly.
3. Use the tape measure to center the template on the back of the screen so the text is facing you.
4. On the front of the screen, use masking tape to mark the edges of the text.
5. Set the template to one side, keeping it close in order to use it as a reference.
6. Starting from the back, use a half cross-stitch to stitch the message on the screen, making sure that all of the stitches are going in the same direction. If you want your message to be a bit bolder, you can use two or even three rows of stitches.
7. The design will be seen from both sides, so it's important to keep your work looking neat. Rather than making knots, secure the thread by tucking it in on itself. Use this method to add new thread.

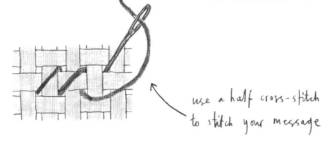

use a half cross-stitch
to stitch your message

Doodled Jars

Perfect for storing office supplies, bathroom essentials, moonshine, whatever...
I mean, who doesn't like fancy jars?

Materials

» **smooth mason jar**
» **paper**
» **extra-fine black paint pen**

Tools

» **scissors**
» **sponge**
» **rubber band**
» **pencil**

What to do

1. Mason jars have a two-layer lid that comes apart so that you can put in your own label. If you can't get hold of one, a normal jar will do. Wash the jar with dishsoap and water to degrease it, and let it dry. Try not to touch it afterwards with dirty fingers.
2. To make a straight line, secure a rubber band around the jar and trace along the band with the paint pen.
3. Carefully doodle on the jar and allow the paint to dry.
4. Unscrew the lid and use a pencil to trace the lid on paper.
5. Decorate this lid insert in a pattern that matches your jar pattern.
6. Cut the circle from the paper, sandwich in the lid, and screw the top back on.

*** Note: Marker is not foodsafe so don't get any on the inside of the jar if you're intending to use it for food.

Rubber band will help you draw a straight line

doodle

your designs all over the jar

PAINT PEN EXTRA FINE

Bird Tree

- -

It's easier for me to justify my slightly crazy obsession with feather birds when they look so pretty.

Materials
» **assorted feathered birds (available at most craft stores)**
» **plain white feathered birds (usually to be found in the floral supply section)**
» **puff paint in assorted colors**
» **twigs in assorted sizes**
» **moss**
» **green floral foam**
» **planter**

Tools
» **exacto knife with sharp blade**

What to do

1. Using puff paint, paint small repeating patterns onto the white birds, allowing the paint to dry in between each layer.
2. Cut the floral foam to snugly fit the planter and place it inside.
3. Secure the twigs in the floral foam.
4. Arrange the moss, making sure to cover the foam and the base of twigs.
5. Attach all the birds to the twigs. The more birds the better!

paint patterns all over the white birds

Botanical Bookends

I'm perpetually on the hunt for bookends, but it's difficult to find any that aren't either crazy expensive or hideously awful. You may have this same problem, so why not make your own?

Materials
» ¾" thick wood
» screws
» black acrylic paint
» white paint pen

Tools
» jigsaw
» safety glasses
» ruler
» pencil
» sandpaper
» wood glue
» drill with bit
» paintbrush
» graphite transfer paper
» floral template
   (see p. 78)

What to do

1. Using a jigsaw and, wearing your safety goggles, cut out four pieces of wood; two pieces measuring 5" x 4½" for the bases and two measuring 5" x 6" for the sides. You can make these ones curved on top, as per the template.
2. Sand down any rough edges.
3. Apply a bead of wood glue to the 5" edge of each base and place the sides on top.
4. On the bottom of each bookend, make two marks approximately 1" from the edge.
5. Drill screws in at each mark, securing the base to the side.
6. Once the wood glue is dry, paint both bookends completely with the black paint and allow to dry.
7. Lay a sheet of graphite transfer paper directly on the bookend (graphite side down) and the floral template (facing up) on top of the graphite paper. Use a pencil to trace the flower, transferring the pattern onto the surface of the bookend.
8. Repeat the transfer for the other bookend.
9. Use the paint pen to carefully trace along the pencil lines with white paint. Allow to dry.

drill screws in to secure

BASE

SIDE

glue side to base

DAVID BELLOS
IS THAT
A Fish IN YOUR EAR
?

PENGUIN BOOKS

WYNDHAM LEWIS
The Apes of God

ISBN 0-14
06.0929

The Medium is the Massage   McLuhan/Fiore

THE HEART OF THE WORLD   NIK COHN

YOU TALKIN' TO ME?   SAM LEITH

P

Valentine Medals

There's a pin back on each, but I think they'd make cute gift toppers – you know, if sporting a medallion isn't really your thing.

- » **1" wood disc (available at craft and DIY stores)**
- » **small wood heart (you can usually get these at craft stores)**
- » **small heart sticker**
- » **black acrylic paint**
- » **⅞" wide ribbon, 12" long**
- » **2 figure-eight jewelry link components**
- » **thread**
- » **2 pin (brooch) backs**

- » **paintbrush**
- » **needle**
- » **iron**
- » **sandpaper**
- » **tacky glue**

What to do

1. Cut the ribbon in half so you have two 6" lengths. Fold each length in half and iron in a crease.
2. Secure the folded ribbon by stitching along each edge.
3. At the creased edge, bring the two sides in to make a triangle. Make a small stitch to secure.
4. Fold down the other end and stitch, making sure any frayed ribbon edges are hidden. Flatten with the iron if necessary.
5. Secure the pin back on top with a stitch or glue, making sure the stitch doesn't show on the front. For the wood heart medal, skip straight to step 9, or for the painted disc medal follow steps 6–8.
6. Place the heart sticker on the center of the wood disc.
7. Paint directly over the sticker (it will act as a resist), and then remove the sticker and discard.
8. Once the disc is dry, lightly sand the edges to remove any stray paint.
9. Stitch the figure-eight jewelry link component to the triangular end of the ribbon.
10. Use tacky glue to attach the figure-eight jewelry link component to the back of the wood and allow to dry.

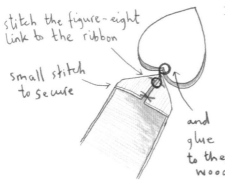

stitch the figure-eight link to the ribbon

small stitch to secure

and glue to the wood

Doorknob Mailbox

Hang this vintage-inspired mailbox on a doorknob and deliver sweet messages to your favorite person through the door on the front. They'll love retrieving your notes through the pull-down door on the side.

Materials

» **cardboard box**
   (I used a photo box)
» **small wood knob**
» **acrylic paint in your**
   choice of colors
» **puff paint**

Tools

» **scissors**
» **paintbrush**
» **ruler**
» **pencil**
» **bone folder**
» **exacto knife and blade**
» **tacky glue**
» **½" circle template**
   (I used a pillbox cap)
» **3" circle template**
   (a cup will do)

What to do

1. To make the door on the front of the box, use a ruler and pencil to lightly draw a 3" high rectangle that is ¾" from each side and 1" from the top.
2. To make the door on the side of the box, use a ruler and pencil to lightly draw a 5" high rectangle that is ½" from each side and ½" from the bottom.
3. Trace the ½" circle template approximately ½" from the top of the side door.
4. On the back of the box, trace the 3" circle template 1" from the top center. This is where the doorknob will slot into the mailbox. Carefully cut it out with the exacto knife.
5. On the side of the box, use the exacto knife to cut the two sides and top of the door, and the circle.
6. On the front of the box, cut the two sides and top of the door.
7. Place the ruler along the bottom of the doors on the front and side, and use the bone folder to score. Gently bend to make the doors open and close.
8. Paint the wood knob and allow to dry.
9. Center the wood knob on the front door and glue. Allow to dry.
10. Decorate the mailbox with acrylic and puff paint and allow to dry.
11. Glue the box closed and allow to dry before hanging the mailbox on a doorknob.

Glue the painted wooden knob to the front door

— CUT
----FOLD

cut a ½" circle in the side door

Butterfly Puppet

When I'm pretending to be the monarch, it flutters around and tickles noses. When my son is pretending to be the monarch, it turns into a rare breed that screeches, has giant claws, and wrecks into his little sister.

Materials

» **orange and black felt**
» **puff paint**
» **thread**
» **cardstock**

Tools

» **printer**
» **scissors**
» **needle**
» **tracing pencil**
» **butterfly template (see p. 79)**

What to do

1. Copy the template onto cardstock and cut out the butterfly shape.
2. Using a tracing pencil, trace two butterflies onto the felt, one orange and one black, and cut them out.
3. Cut a small semicircle out of the remaining black felt.
4. Use a needle and thread to stitch the semicircle onto the back of the orange butterfly.
5. Use the tracing pencil to draw a butterfly design on the back of the black felt. I drew freehand teardrop shapes, but you can make any pattern you wish.
6. Cut small slits in the middle of each teardrop shape to get it started and trim outwards to the edges to make it neat.
7. Lay the two butterfly shapes together, making sure that the semicircle shape is on the outside/back before you sew the two shapes together.
8. Using a simple running stitch, sew along the edge to join the two shapes together. if they do not line up perfectly, carefully trim along the edge with a pair of nail-scissors.
10. Make spots on the black felt (butterfly front) with puff paint and allow to dry.

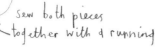

sew both pieces together with a running

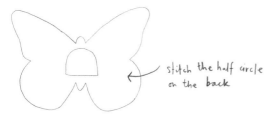

stitch the half circle on the back

Templates

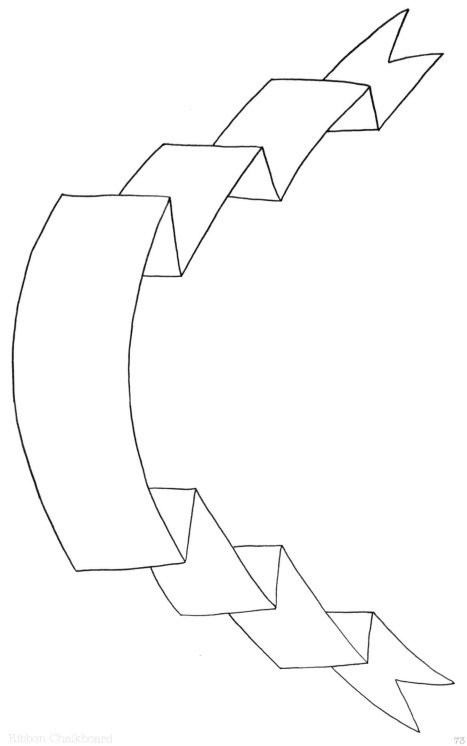

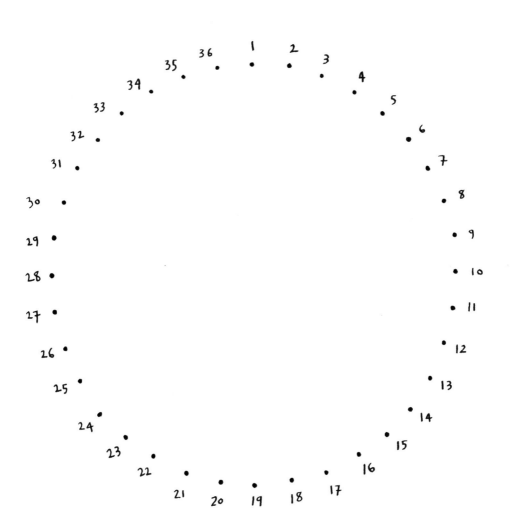

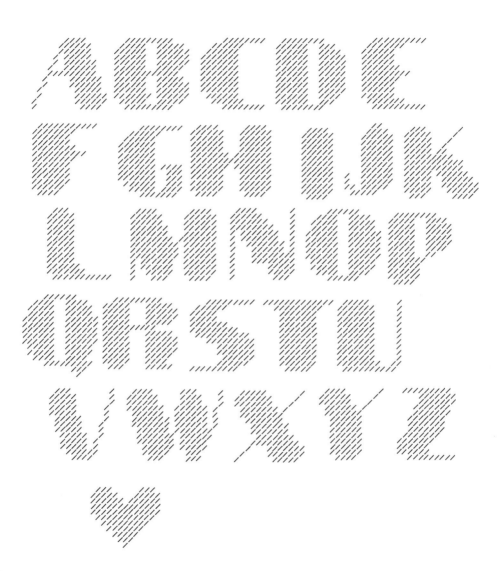

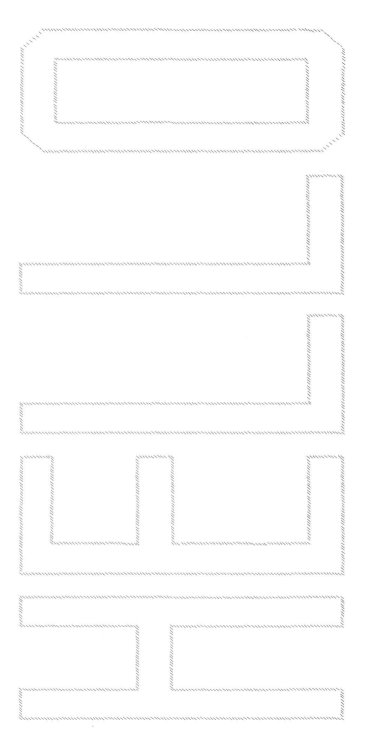

Acknowledgements
This book is affectionately dedicated to my three
very favorite people: Isla, Emmett, and Phil. Special
thanks to my parents, brothers, and grandparents,
with love and appreciation for a lifetime filled with
encouragement. Cheers to my incredible friends,
most particularly Kris, Rach, Em, Sage, Amy, Alisia
and Renee. And a million thanks to my thoughtful,
creative, fabulous readers: without you (and a very
patient, talented editor named Ziggy), this wouldn't
have happened. Thank you!

Published by Cicada Books Limited

Written by Abbey Hendrickson
Edited by Ziggy Hanaor
Designed by Lisa Sjukur and Sandra Zellmer for April
Photography by Garry Maclennan
Illustration by Fiona Biddington

British Library Cataloguing-in-Publication Data.

A CIP record for this book
is available from the British Library.
ISBN: 978-1-908714-00-8

© 2012 Cicada Books Limited

Cicada Books Limited
48 Burghley Road
London, NW5 1UE
United Kingdom

E: ziggy@cicadabooks.co.uk
W: www.cicadabooks.co.uk

Printed in China